OUR
TIME
TOGETHER

OUR TIME TOGETHER

JIM & DORIS MORENTZ

Abingdon Press
Nashville

Our Time Together

Copyright © 1983 by Abingdon Press

Library of Congress Cataloging in Publication Data

Morentz, Jim.
Our time together.
1. Children's sermons.   2. Christian education—
Audio-visual aids.   I. Morentz, Doris, 1929-   II. Title.
BV4315.M628   1983   252'.53   83-6349

ISBN-0-687-29775-3

MANUFACTURED BY THE PARTHENON PRESS AT
NASHVILLE, TENNESSEE, UNITED STATES OF AMERICA

To Jim and Deb who taught us everything we know about children—especially the joys of being parents.

Contents

Introduction

The majority of the sermons in this book consists of various series paralleling the seasons of the church year. Prior to each series is an introduction that indicates the things that you will need. In addition to these objects there will also appear on each Sunday a key word. This word is to be an integral part of the story. Often these words may be difficult for the children to understand. If that is true, there is a simple explanation of the word to make sure the children understand it. This is a good plan for using the proper word and educating the children, rather than speaking down to them. We hope to bring them up to a new understanding. A little education each week adds up to a lot of learning over the whole year.

Use your imagination. Put yourself into the lesson. Have fun and make it fun for the children. Remember, you may have some great ideas to improve on what we have done; do it your way. Good luck.

Suggestions and Prejudices of the Authors

This is not an introduction in the typical sense. In reality, we sat down and came up with a few of the things we dislike most about children's sermons. This is a result of listening to presentations of children's sermons from border to border and coast to coast, and reading many others. In order to make this introduction a little more readable, and a better learning opportunity for you, the pastor and presenter, these negatives have been turned into positives. It is hoped that you will be able to use some of them and find them helpful in your preparation.

Try to get the children up front. Invite them to come forward during a hymn, indicating this is the time for the children to present themselves in the altar area. If they come forward during the singing of a hymn there should be little interruption of the service.

Never insist that children come. If you notice children who have not come forward when the invitation is given, just let them sit. Don't embarrass them. They will eventually feel confident enough to join the others.

In all probability you have a predominant age in your group of children who come for the children's sermon. Find out what that age group is, and aim your sermons at them. It is always much easier if you know the age span you are primarily talking to.

When the children come forward, make sure that you arrange them in such a way that you are still facing the congregation. When you turn your back on the congregation during the children's sermon, it is exclusionary. You do not want to ignore the congregation during the children's sermon, you are just trying to include the children in the service.

Don't expect answers. If you constantly ask questions and demand answers, you'll frighten some of the children. You will also give the extroverts too much opportunity to dominate.

If you do ask a question and receive an answer, consider it a bonus, but never plan this sermon around the necessity of getting an answer to any question.

You will notice in this book that some objects used in certain lessons are given a name. The object will be the presenter for a period of weeks so the children will begin to recognize the object as the presenter.

Be sure to explain clearly what the object is, the role it will play, and how it will be the presenter during this period of the object lessons.

Get the children involved with the objects. Stand up and say, "This is Herman the Hammer. Say good-morning to Herman." Let the children call out, "Good morning, Herman!" It is a great way to get them involved.

Practice the demonstrations. Many times there will be opportunities to do something a little bit delicate. Do not take a chance. Don't think you know it, but practice the demonstration first.

Be a ham. Your children will love it. They will also relate to it. Some of the parents may think you are overdoing it, but remember it's a children's sermon. That is the audience you are talking to, the audience you are trying to teach. Don't be afraid to ham it up.

Big buildings lead to big lessons learned. Don't be afraid to build it up and build it up, so that when the final object illustration comes, the children are ready. They will be excited about it and waiting for it.

Some of these lessons will call for the participation of one or more of the children. Pick the children carefully. Make sure that they are well rehearsed so that it becomes an excellent learning experience instead of an embarrassment.

As you are going through the lesson, observe the children's eyes, because in them you will see reflected their interest and involvement, or their boredom. They will show you how you are doing.

We are not quite certain who first started using children's sermons, but are willing to guess that it was the circuit rider who never preached at the same church twice in his life. We pity the pastor who is celebrating his twenty-fifth anniversary—the difficulty he has had coming up with twenty-five years of new and interesting sermons. But coming up with new children's sermons each Sunday must have driven him out of his mind. We hope that this book is helpful to you and makes your life a little easier for the year of this series.

Advent
(Four Sundays)

Our first series is Advent. We begin with a new year's celebration. This is to introduce the fact that this is the first Sunday of the church year, so it's a happy new year.

The rest of Advent is based on the theme of light. This is a very appropriate theme to lead up to Christmas.

Don't get spoiled by the small list of objects required, it won't always be this easy!

Objects Required

- noisemaker or hat for New Year's Eve party
- light bulb
- candle and matches

Gospel Lesson: Matthew 24:37-44
Key Word: **Watch**
Object: Noisemaker or New Year's Eve party hat

Happy New Year! (At this point, take the noisemaker and start, if it's a horn, blow it; if you have a hat, put it on. Then again say Happy New Year.) It's sort of funny to have me wish you a happy new year today. It's not even December, so of course it cannot be New Years Day. I guess you are wondering why the pastor is saying Happy New Year! We all know that the new year comes after Christmas.

Today is the First Sunday of Advent. Do you know what the first Sunday of Advent means? It means the coming of Christ into the world. That's what Advent means, and that's what we are celebrating today. That is why today is the first day of the new year in the church; because this is the beginning of the celebration of Christ's coming into the world.

Some of you may have a little brother or sister. If you do, maybe you can remember back to when your mommy and daddy were getting ready for your sister or brother to arrive and move into your household. I am sure you remember how they went out and bought a crib and set the crib up. They bought blankets, diapers, and a high chair. They had to get a playpen. Some of these things they borrowed from neighbors, and some they bought new. All of this did not suddenly happen; your mom and dad had to get ready for it. This took a lot of time. For some of you the baby may have moved into its own room. And for others, your new brother or sister may have moved into your room, and that made it a little bit crowded. But you've gotten along fine.

Now we are getting ready for Advent and the coming of the Christ Child when he had to move into a new room too, but his room wasn't quite as fancy as yours. That is what we will be talking about for the four Sundays of Advent—the coming of the Christ Child.

Let's talk about our key word. Our key word for the First Sunday of Advent is *watch* (hold up your wristwatch). Not this kind of a watch, not the kind of watch that tells the time; but the kind of watch that means "keep your eyes open," "don't stop looking, or you'll miss something."

I am sure many of you may have gone to a Thanksgiving Day parade where Santa Claus came to town, or you may have been to stores or the mall where they are starting to get all decorated for Christmas. All the people who plan on selling toys and all sorts of other things for Christmas are not missing out, they are getting ready, they're watching, they are not going to let it sneak by. That is the world. We are the church, so surely if the world is getting ready for Christmas, you boys and girls and your mommies and daddies should be getting ready for Christmas too. So, don't forget, keep your eyes open, don't stop looking, don't miss anything, because you have to keep watching to see what happens on Christmas Eve. It is going to come very quickly now. So, keep watching and Happy New Year from the church as we look forward to a happy Christmas.

Gospel Lesson: Matthew 3:1-12
Key Word: **Repent**
Object: Light bulb

Today is the Second Sunday in Advent, and I am going to use a word that many of you may not understand. Our word today is *repent.* That is a strange word, and I don't believe you know what it means, do you? Before I tell you what it means, I would like to tell you why we are using that particular word.

These sermons for you children will each have a key word, and each will always have an object. One of the reasons I like these sermons is that instead of using a very simple key word that is easy for little children to understand, I'll take a word that is an adult person's word and then explain it to you so you can understand what it means when you hear it again. By the time this year is over, you will know a whole lot of new words—grown-up words—and you will be able to understand them too.

So, today our word is repent. Repent means "to be sorry for a sin," "to be sorry we did wrong." During these next few weeks when you go shopping with your mom or dad, almost every place you go will be crowded. When you go shopping with your parents they usually tell you to stay close to them. Have you ever wandered off, and all of a sudden you turned around and could not find them? They were gone. You got scared! You looked around and they were nowhere in sight. Then all of a sudden you saw your mom or dad and ran over to them and said, "Oh, am I glad I found you." That's what repent means. It means you got lost from Jesus, you got scared, and you are sorry.

One of the interesting things about getting lost is that you are not lost until you know you're lost. When you wander off from your mom and dad, and you don't notice that they are out of sight or that you have lost them, you are fine. But once you find out you are lost, then you get scared. That's what happened in our gospel lesson today. Many of the people to whom John the Baptist was preaching did not even know they were lost, so he was like a voice crying in the wilderness saying, "You're lost from Jesus. You are lost from the Messiah, and you don't care. Repent! Feel sorry! Be afraid! Look for him and you will find him" (hold up the light bulb.) See this light bulb? It is just like all the rest of the light bulbs that light up this church, except it is dark and it is cold. Do you know why? Right now it isn't connected to anything that you can plug in. There is no current to make the bulb light up. The people that John the Baptist was preaching to were like that. They didn't know the Messiah had come, so they were walking around like cold, dark bulbs, saying, "Some day the Messiah will come, and we'll get plugged in." And what John the Baptist was saying was, "Repent! Look, the Messiah is here." That's what the story is telling us today. If you've lost your connection to Jesus, be sorry, be afraid, look around for your light cord because you know the light cord is here, and the current is here, and you know how you can get plugged in again, and you know how you can light up your life.

Gospel Lesson: Matthew 11:2-11
Key Word: **Go**
Object: Candle

You remember last Sunday I told you we are going to have a key word and it will be a big word that you may not be able to understand, but it would be explained? Well, here I am this Sunday with a key word that you can all understand. This morning the key word is *go.*

I am sure you know this word because one day your mom or dad said, do this or do that, and you didn't move fast enough, and they lost their patience with you and said, "Go!" I'm sure you know what go means!

As we get closer and closer to Christmas, all the Christmas decorations are up everywhere. John the Baptist in our gospel lesson today is still preaching and saying, "The Messiah has come! The Messiah has come!" John the Baptist had a lot of people following him. Many people had been staying with him in a little camp out in the wilderness. They were called his disciples or his friends. John the Baptist finds out that Jesus is nearby, and he sends some of his friends to ask Jesus, "Are you the Messiah, or is there somebody else?" That was a very simple question. "Just give me a yes or no—Are you the Messiah?" This is one of the few times in the Bible when Jesus gets a little irritated, a little upset. You remember one time he threw the money changers out of the temple when he got angry because they were using the house of God for selling sacrifices to the people coming to the temple. Well, this is another case where Jesus got a little upset. Instead of saying, "Yes, I am the Messiah," (he thought John the Baptist, his cousin, should have known), he showed his irritation and that he was a little angry. When they said, "Are you really the Messiah?" He didn't say, "Yes, Go tell John I really am." He said, "Go tell John what you see. The blind see, the lame walk, the deaf hear, and the dead come to life." That was the only answer he gave. He didn't say, "Yes, I am the Messiah." He said, "Go and tell John what I have done, and then he will believe." The things that are easiest to believe, are the things we have seen. So Jesus said, "Go and tell John what you have seen, and he will know."

Now we are going to take this candle (hold it up) and call it our John the Baptist candle. Our John the Baptist candle announces that the light of the world has come, and so we will take our John the Baptist candle, but we won't light it. Instead we will save the candle until next week, and next week we will see what happens to the John the Baptist candle, as John continues to proclaim the Messiah is coming.

FOURTH SUNDAY IN ADVENT

Gospel Lesson: Matthew 1:18-25
Key Word: **Immanuel**
Objects: Candle and matches

I guess we should explain a little something about our key word today, which is *Immanuel.* It is sort of funny, isn't it, that in the gospel lesson we heard "His name shall be called Immanuel." But when Jesus was born, they didn't call him Immanuel, they called him Jesus. A little bit earlier in the gospel lesson Joseph was told by the angel, "You shall call his name Jesus." But everything that happens through the whole Christmas story, and very often during Jesus' entire lifetime, is a part of the Old Testament being fulfilled—that means "happening"—just the way the prophets of the Old Testament said it would. So here we see the Old Testament quoted, ". . . call his name Immanuel." Now why should they call him Immanuel? Because Immanuel means "God with us." Jesus means "God will save." The angel said to Joseph, "You shall call his name Jesus." And this fulfilled the Old Testament prediction, "He shall be called Immanuel, God with us." So Jesus was God coming to earth to visit and save his people. That is how it started, with just that little baby with those two big names—Jesus and Immanuel, God with us.

You see what has happened now? In this last Sunday of Advent we no longer have John preaching in the wilderness and saying, "Make straight the way, the Messiah is coming." We now have the angel announcing, "Jesus will be born." So we now take our John the Baptist candle from last week—remember we didn't light the John the Baptist candle because the light had not come. But now, with the announcement of the angel, that Immanuel, God with us, is arriving in the form of that little baby, Jesus, we take the John the Baptist candle and light it, and it becomes the fulfillment. It now becomes the Jesus candle.

Christmas

(Christmas and two Sundays after)

This series includes a Christmas sermon for Christmas Eve or Day, depending on when you have your service. The two Sundays after Christmas are also included.

Objects Required

- mother and small baby
- pair of sneakers or running shoes
- sign—on one side will be printed
    word, on the other side *Word*
    (one all small letters; one with
    a capital *W*)

CHRISTMAS EVE OR CHRISTMAS DAY

Gospel Lesson: Luke 2:1-20
Key Word: **Baby**
Object: Have a mother with a small baby come up
front and stand next to the pastor during the
children's sermon.

Well, it is finally Christmas Day (or Christmas Eve). All the malls are empty now. All the stores are starting to take down their Christmas displays. Pretty soon the stores will be running after-Christmas specials, and you can go in and buy everything cheaper. Christmas just sort of comes to an end Christmas Day. Isn't that a shame? Because to those of us who are Christians, Christmas Day is only the beginning. This is the day we celebrate the birth of our Savior, which means the beginning of our lives, and the beginning of the year, not the end.

Now that it is Christmas Day (or Eve) what do you think we could have for a key word, and what do you think our object should be? Well I just don't know anything better than *Baby.* (Have the mother and child come up front and stand with the pastor. If it should happen there is no baby in the congregation, use a doll. If the baby is quiet and asleep, the pastor can say, "See how quietly our baby sleeps. Just the way Jesus slept in the manger on that first Christmas Eve." If the baby happens to be gurgling or crying, the pastor can say, "See how our baby is alive and kicking and crying. I'm sure the baby Jesus had those times when he was born and lying in a manger too. You just cry all you want and let those lungs grow nice and strong. I'll just talk a little louder.")

I'm going to tell you boys and girls a little secret. Most of the men I know think all babies look alike; but women almost never think that. Most of them can always tell the difference. I don't really know why that is. But the baby that was born in the manger in Bethlehem was certainly different. What really makes babies different? Let me tell you what happened on that first Christmas. Some shepherds were in the field, and an angel came to them and said, "Jesus is born." They soon left their sheep because they believed and went down to see the new Christ Child.

Weeks before that, a star had appeared, and three wise men from the East believed it was a sign of the birth of Jesus. They also left on a long journey to visit the Christ Child. Those people, so many years ago, knew that that baby was different. And today, as we look at this little baby here, next to me, that baby is different to its mother and father just as the baby that Mary had that night so long ago was different for all of us. He came to save the world. He came as Immanuel—God with us. And so today (tonight) we have to show the same faith the shepherds showed; we have to show the same faith the wise men showed when they said, "We will go to the manger to worship the new king." Today (Tonight) that is our job, to show the faith and to say, "Surely Christ is with us."

FIRST SUNDAY AFTER CHRISTMAS

Gospel Lesson: Matthew 2:13-15, 19-23
Key Word: **Flee**
Object: Pair of sneakers or running shoes

Our key word today is *flee.*Do you know what it means to flee? Let me give you a little help (hold up running shoes or sneakers). Isn't it funny, when you put on your sneakers, you just feel as if you are going to be able to run fast. You wear your sneakers when you go out to play baseball or basketball; anytime you want to be able to run fast you want to have on your sneakers.

And that's what flee means. Flee means "to run away." Now this is not the kind of a flea that gets on your dog and makes it scratch. That's a different kind of flea. This is the kind of flee that means to run away.

I am sure a lot of you know one of those kids at school who is always picking on everybody. When you see him coming your way, and you know he's going to start trouble, you flee. That means you run away. You head for safety. Sometimes you may run into the school, or sometimes you may run home, but you don't want to be where that big bully can catch you.

Well, that is just what Mary and Joseph did in the lesson today. Herod, who was the big bully, was afraid of the little baby Jesus. He had heard the people wanted Jesus as their king. When Herod heard about this, he sent his soldiers to find and kill Jesus. Now, God just does not allow those kinds of things to happen to his Son. He sent an angel to Joseph and Mary and said, "Flee! Run away, stay away until King Herod is dead." So Joseph took Mary and the baby Jesus, and they went to

Egypt. They stayed in Egypt a long time—until the bad King Herod was dead.

Why do you think God had to hide his Son and let him run away? If God is able to do anything, why didn't he just protect Jesus? Well, there are two reasons. Do you remember at Christmastime when we said sometimes Jesus did things to make the Old Testament come true. This is another one of those times, and in the gospel lesson today it says, "Out of Egypt have I called my son." And so, Mary and Joseph fled to Egypt taking the baby with them. There he grew and had a chance to become a strong young man. Jesus needed time to grow. As a little baby he certainly couldn't stand up against the scribes and the Pharisees and the priests. He had to grow to become strong. Then he would be ready to take his stand, but for now, he had to flee.

SECOND SUNDAY AFTER CHRISTMAS

Gospel Lesson: John 1:1-18
Key Word: **Word**
Object: A sign—on one side of the sign is *Word* (capital *W);* on the other side is *word* (small *w)*

I am certain you know by now that all the children's sermons are about the gospel lessons. And boy! that gospel lesson today was a tough one! Did you boys and girls have trouble following it? Well, don't feel bad. I am sure many grown-ups had trouble with it too. Now let us see if there is a way we can make this lesson clearer.

I am going to play a trick on you. I am going to fool you right in front of your eyes. I need two children to help me (select two from the congregation).

Fine. Now here I have a sign, and I want you to give me a word, any word at all. (You will probably be given words like dog, cat, house, mom, dad, boy, girl.) That's right. That's right. They are all words. They are good words. And what does "word" mean? A word is a term that represents an object or an idea. That is what a word does.

Now just watch this. Here is where I am going to play a trick on you—right in front of your eyes. I am going to take the sign from ——— (name child) and hand it to ——— (name other child)—turn the sign around so that *Word* with the capital *W* is showing).

Now I am going to ask again. Somebody give me a word. What does this mean? (Again, you will probably hear dog, cat, etc.) No. See that is the trick. When we had "word" with the little or small *w,* that means dog, cat, mouse, or boy or girl. (turn the sign back to small *w* at this point). Now, here is the trick again (turn the sign with the capital *W* showing). *Word* with a capital *W* comes right out of our gospel lesson. Are you ready? "And the Word became flesh." That means that Jesus is the living Word, capital *W.* So, if you look in the Bible, God always is a capital *G;* Jesus always a capital *J.* When you see Word with a capital *W,* that means God.

Here it is boys and girls. (turn the sign to the small *w word)* With the little *w* this means things and ideas (turn the sign around so that the capital *W Word* shows.) This means God. That is what our gospel lesson said today. "The Word became flesh . . . ." Jesus is the new Word for the New Testament.

Epiphany
(Eight Sundays)

This series again has a first Sunday that is a very special day and is treated as such. The other Sundays follow.

First Sunday: The Baptism of our Lord: A small bowl of water.

The Epiphany of our Lord: A star (this sermon is for those who have a special service on the day of Epiphany, January 6).

The Second through the Eighth Sundays after the Epiphany are all under the theme of "Tell" or "Communication."

Objects Required

- star
- water
- telegram
- newspaper
- Bible
- TV set or *TV Guide*
- box of candy
- comics page
- mail order catalog

THE EPIPHANY OF OUR LORD

Gospel Lesson: Matthew 2:1-12
Key Word: **Epiphany**
Object: Star

We thought Christmas was over. Now here, all of a sudden, three weeks after Christmas, we come to the Christmas story again. The gospel lesson was about the three wise men coming to see Jesus, who was lying in a manger, in a little stable in Bethlehem. Now, I thought all that happened on Christmas Eve. You remember, don't you? Some of the Christmas cards you received had a picture of the shepherds and the wise men, and it seemed to me that they were all there at the same time, gathered around the manger.

Well, now here it is written in the Bible, so it must be true that the wise men came and brought their gifts of gold, frankincense, and myrrh. That's the same as the story I remember. But here it is, not Christmas Eve, not the night Jesus was born, but a few weeks later. I guess we all better take a look at our key word to see what *Epiphany* means.

Who knows what *Epiphany* means? Does anyone know? Well, I guess I had better tell you. And you mothers and fathers should listen too, because you might learn something.

With a capital *E* and with a small *e,* Epiphany means two different things. You remember a few weeks ago we talked about the word "word"? Remember? We held up the sign with *w-o-r-d* with a small *w,* and we said that names things and ideas. Then we held up the sign with *W-o-r-d* with a capital *W,* and we said that means "God."

Now we have Epiphany, with both a capital *E* and a

small *e*. Epiphany with a capital *E* means "the twelfth day," or twelve days after Christmas, which is January 6. January 6 is the day of Epiphany. Now when epiphany has a small *e* it means the "appearance of a god." Do you see how they tie together? Twelve days after Christmas, the appearance of a god. Now, here's the star that the three wise men followed, and this is the Epiphany, twelve days after Christmas with a capital *E*. That is what Epiphany is—the appearance of God twelve days after Christmas, leading the wise men by a star to worship the baby Jesus. That is what Epiphany is. Happy Epiphany to you all.

THE BAPTISM OF OUR LORD
(First Sunday after the Epiphany)

Gospel Lesson: Matthew 3:13-17
Key Word: **Baptized**
Object: Water

Today in the gospel lesson we heard about Jesus being *baptized.* Have you ever seen a baptism? We do it all the time right here in our church. It is one of the most amazing things that happens right before your very eyes. I wonder if you have any idea what really happens?

I saw a magician the other day on television. He did some really great tricks. I could not figure out how he did them. In one trick he put a woman in a trunk, closed the lid, and when he opened the trunk again, there was a lion cub inside. Then he closed the trunk again, and when he opened it this time, the lady was back inside. I thought that was a pretty amazing trick, and I couldn't figure out how he did it.

Well, boys and girls, let me tell you, there has never been a magician performing on the stage who did anything like the miracle that takes place in baptism, right here in our church. See this water? This water can make you clean all over your body—inside your body and outside your body. It can also change your name. All this happens at the same time, and it only takes a few seconds.

When this water is placed on you, in the name of God the Father, God the Son, and God the Holy Spirit, it makes you clean. It also makes your name Christian. God will say to you, "This is my child in whom I am well pleased." That is the miracle of baptism, and that is something no magician can ever do. No matter how fancy a magician's trick is, he can never outperform God!

This First Sunday of Epiphany is all about the baptism of Jesus. Because that is so special, this children's sermon was about water. For the rest of the Epiphany season we will be talking about communications. That is a big word that we will talk more about later.

SECOND SUNDAY AFTER THE EPIPHANY

Gospel Lesson: John 1:29-41
Key Word: **Messiah**
Object: Telegram

For the next few weeks we are going to be talking about how to tell the story of God and Jesus. Every Sunday for the next few weeks we are going to have a different kind of object to help us understand the story a little better. There will be all sorts of different ways to tell the story, and today we are going to start by using a telegram.

For thousands of years the Jewish nation has been waiting for the Messiah. Can you imagine, for thousands of years, waiting for God to come? That is what the Jewish nation had to do, and they are still doing it. Waiting and waiting and waiting. Remember last Sunday in the gospel lesson we talked about John baptizing Jesus? Here today, Jesus is ready to be a minister. John makes the announcement. He says, "I saw the Spirit descend on him and it stayed. This is the Son of God."

For the next few weeks we will be showing how we can spread the Word—the news (have a child bring the telegram up to the pastor). Great! Here is the first way we could spread the news—by telegram. Let's read it. You know, you don't see telegrams very much these days. Telegrams used to be one of the best ways to send the news, but now everybody uses the telephone, television, newspapers, etc.

But telegrams are still used, and here is one right now.

Are you ready for this? Here is the big news. This is from Andrew to his brother Simon Peter, and now, after thousands of years of waiting, it says: "We have found the Messiah, the Christ." You see, that is our word for today, *Messiah. Messiah* means "Jesus," "the Christ." We have found the Messiah after waiting all these thousands of years. That is pretty exciting news. And that is our story for today.

Gospel Lesson: Matthew 4:12-23
Key Words: **Follow Me**
Object: Newspaper

Remember last week we had a telegram that told us the Messiah has come—that Jesus is here? Now this week Jesus is starting his ministry. We have a newspaper to help us this week (have a child bring up a newspaper).

Now Jesus didn't have all these ways to tell the news when he was here on earth, going around preaching. The newspaper headline says, *"Follow Me."* That is what Jesus said.

Let us play Jesus and his disciples (pastor marches around the church picking out children and saying to them by name, "_____ follow me. _____, follow me," until he finally returns to the front of the church). That is how the news got around in the days when Jesus was preaching. He walked and talked to several men, and then he said, "Follow me." That is how Jesus picked his disciples, and that is how they followed him.

Now we have telegrams and newspapers to help us tell the story. Remember, boys and girls, Jesus did not stop calling people; he is still doing it today. Right here, right now. He is still saying to you, "Follow me."

FOURTH SUNDAY AFTER THE EPIPHANY

Gospel Lesson: Matthew 5:1-12
Key Word: **Listen**
Object: Bible

We have had a telegram. We have had a newspaper. Now wait until you see what we have this week. It is a book, not just any book. This is the Bible. Now there are thousands and thousands of books. Some of them bring us information, and some of them are just fun to read. This is a special message and a special book. This is God's Word right from him.

Now, do you know what our word for today is? It is *listen*. Let me tell you why you have to listen to this especially well. This is not like the Ten Commandments. This doesn't say you must do this, or you must not do that. This says if you want to enjoy life, and you want to have fun, and you want to please God then you will be humble, be kind, be gentle, be pure, be peaceful, be good, be happy. Are you listening? I told you you would have to listen very carefully, because God is telling you this is what you have to do if you want to have a good life and love God. You can be all these things because God loves you first. That is what it says in his book, the Bible.

The Bible brings you the good news that God loves you first.

FIFTH SUNDAY AFTER THE EPIPHANY

Gospel Lesson: Matthew 5:13-20
Key Word: **Light**
Object: *TV Guide* or TV section of newspaper or, if
   possible, a TV set

Now, we have had a telegram, we have had a newspaper, and we have even had the Bible. Now we have television. Did you ever get all set to watch your favorite television show? You get the popcorn, you get the soda, and you are all set, only to find out after you are all settled down that the TV set is not working. Just so you don't think there is something wrong with you when you get angry about a broken set, let me tell you, your pastor gets angry, too. And so do Mom and Dad. When you are all set to have a special treat, and suddenly you find out the television set doesn't work, and your special treat isn't going to happen, or you are not going to see your football game, that's enough to get you upset.

Well, without that *light* for the picture tube, all you have is a blank piece of glass. That is really no fun. Before you get upset, let me tell you that the plug just came out. OK? Let's put the plug back in; now we will turn on the set.

That is what Jesus was talking about in the Gospel for today. Turn it on. Let your light shine. Don't hide it! Hold it up high so all the kinds at school can see you are one of Jesus' own children. Let your light shine. The smile on your face, the care you show for your friends can say loud and clear, I am one of His own. I let my light shine. I'm turned on. I'm plugged in. I am going to enter the kingdom of heaven.

SIXTH SUNDAY AFTER THE EPIPHANY

Gospel Lesson: Matthew 5:20-37
Key Word: **Love**
Object: A box of candy

The gospel lesson today is a very hard lesson. I think it is much easier for adults to understand than children. For your sermon I picked a different subject. We will talk about love. Jesus often talked to his disciples about love.

We have been talking all about telling and communication in this Epiphany series. So far we have used a telegram, newspaper, Bible, and a TV set. After all that I thought I was beginning to understand what communications were, and here we are with a box of candy. (Hold up the candy box for all to see.)

That has nothing to do with communications.

Jesus tells his disciples a really far-out thing. He says, "*Love* your enemy. If someone robs you, give him more. If some hits you, turn the other cheek, but don't hit back."

I said this is far out, and I mean far out! You just can't do that. If you did, people would walk all over you. Your friends would eat your lunch, take your bike, beat you up, and you would have a pretty unhappy life.

Jesus is not telling us to let the world or our friends push us around. He is saying that if you love him you have to be different from most other people.

When people look at Jesus' disciples they should be able to see a difference; they are not like the rest of the world.

You act as if you love, because you do love. God loved you first, so we love other people.

At Christmas, at birthdays, on Valentine's Day—oh, boy! that's a big one—we often give someone we love a box of candy. That does quite a job of communicating. You give the message, "I Love You," all tied up in a nice box of candy.

A box of candy surely does tell a story. It says, "I Love You."

SEVENTH SUNDAY AFTER THE EPIPHANY

Gospel Lesson: Matthew 5:38-48
Key Word: **Perfect**
Object: Page of comics

We have had a telegram, a newspaper, the Bible, television, and today the comics page from a newspaper. I guess most of you who can read, read the comics. If you can't read, you look at the pictures, or your mom or dad reads the comics to you. The comics are really neat. You know some are even for adults? Children love "Peanuts," so do parents. Then there is a comic called "Doonesbury." It's right there in the comics, but it's for adults. Sometimes I can't even understand it.

When I was young, they called these "funny papers." They don't do that much any more. Do you know why? Not many of them are too funny. Some are all about the bad boys; some are all about the bad girls. Some are history stories, some are just plain bad. Then again, some are still funny.

We got so involved in the funnies, we almost forgot our word for today. It is *perfect*. What is a perfect funny paper? A comic that is funny. I like "Peanuts," it is always funny. It is a perfect comic. It is supposed to be funny, and it is funny. That makes it perfect.

Jesus told us today, right at the end of the Gospel,

"You therefore must be perfect." What makes you perfect? When you are good, you know what that means. (Point to the comics.) You must be funny. (Take the page from the child and point to the child.) You must be good. It's just that simple. Try to be perfect this week. The comics can carry a message. It is another way, in Jesus' modern world, that we can communicate.

EIGHTH SUNDAY AFTER THE EPIPHANY

Gospel Lesson: Matthew 6:24-34
Key Word: **Anxious**
Object: Mail order catalog

We have had a telegram, a newspaper, the Bible, television, the funnies, a box of candy, and now—here is a mail order catalog. I know you get these at your house. There seems to be no way to stop them from coming. They come every day, all year long. Some people like me never open them; we just toss them in the wastebasket. I know people who pile them up when they are too busy to look at them and wait until they have enough time. Then they read every item. They get out their pen and stamps and start sending orders for all sorts of things. They just love it. They just love to use that mail order catalog. I know a woman who buys everything out of these catalogs except her groceries, and if she could do that, I really think she would.

Let me tell you what the people who sent this catalog to me hoped to do. Our word for today is *anxious.* They want me to be anxious for some of the things for sale in this book. They want me to want the item so badly I just have to order it. That is not what Jesus said in our Gospel today. He said, "Don't be anxious. You don't need all these things." You know though, there are some things alike between this book (hold up the catalog) and this book (hold up the Bible). Some people and companies send out millions of these and hope to make some people so anxious they will buy something. This book, (hold up the Bible) is printed in the millions every year and given to people in the hope that it will make them less anxious. It can help them to believe that God, who takes care of all living things, can take care of you too. You do not have to be anxious. You have this book.

LAST SUNDAY AFTER THE EPIPHANY

Gospel Lesson: Matthew 17:1-9
Key Words: **Tell** and **Communication**
Objects: All the communication objects from previous Sundays, held by the children, lined up across the front of the church.

Here you see all the things we have talked about these last few weeks. There's the telegram, the newspaper, the Bible, the TV, the comics page, the box of candy, the catalog, and this week—nothing.

This week I want to tell you what has really been happening these last several weeks. Our key words— and we have two of them today—are *tell* and *communication.*These are two separate words, but they mean the same. To the young folks we say, "You have to tell the story." To the older folks we might say, "You have to communicate the story."

Every one of the objects we have had suggests a way of telling or communicating the story. Somebody has to start by telling the story, by writing it, or showing it on TV, or reporting it in newspapers. Now we come to the problem of all the stories you see or hear in these things (point to the objects the children are holding).

What do you believe? What do you believe? Believe the witnesses, the ones who saw it happen. They will tell it with such conviction that you can believe them. Peter, James, and John saw Jesus transformed. That means he was "changed." They heard God say, "This is my beloved Son, with whom I am well pleased." They were the communicators. They saw it. They believed it, and they told the story with such conviction that we believe it too. You can be transformed into a communicator today. Go tell what you believe with such conviction that all the other children will believe you too.

Jesus loves you. That is the story you have to tell with conviction.

Lenten Introduction

The Lenten Series (seven Sundays) introduces Herman the Hammer. It is important that you believe in Herman and that he can help you establish contact with the children. Dress up Herman—face, moustache, anything you choose to make him a little more real to the children.

What we are trying to do is establish Herman the Hammer as the pastor's assistant. To work with Herman there are about a dozen additional very simple objects. They are easy to obtain and to use.

This is the list of materials needed:

Objects Required

- a hammer to be called Herman the Hammer, the instructor, during the entire seven-week series.
- two-by-four board, twelve inches long.
- hand-printed sign that says, I who speak to you am he
- small tack and a place to put the tack
- nail (eight penny, which will be driven about one-half inch into the board)
- a blindfold
- piece of string
- pair of scissors
- small nail (four penny)
- 3 quarter-inch lattice strip boards, one inch to two inches wide, twelve inches long
- handful of palm fronds
- cymbal, triangle, or little bell

FIRST SUNDAY IN LENT

Gospel Lesson: Matthew 4:1-11
Key Word: **Firm**
Objects: Herman the Hammer
Two-by-four board, twelve inches long

Since this is the first Sunday in Lent, I would like to introduce you to our new assistant to the pastor. Our new assistant will be helping me teach for the six Sundays in Lent, and also for Easter.

This is Herman the Hammer. Boys and girls, say good morning to our friend Herman the Hammer.

Each Sunday Herman will have a message for you, and so will I. I would like to begin my part of the message by reminding you about the gospel lesson for the day. Remember in the gospel lesson the devil tried to tempt Jesus? No matter what he tried to offer, Jesus stood *firm* and said no.

Now it is very important for us to know exactly what the word "firm" means. The way I just used it is almost as good a way to explain firm as you can find. When you say, "I want to go out," and your mother or father says no, that is being firm. When you say, "Please, please, please may I go out?" and they say No, that is being very firm. In the story today, Jesus was firm when he was first tempted by the devil and then, when the devil tempted him again, he was very firm.

These stories in the Bible are not there just to entertain us. They are there to help us. This story says to us: "When you know that you have a chance to do something wrong, or someone tries to get you to do something wrong, you have to remember the story of the way Jesus was tempted, the way Jesus stood firm and said no." All through life it will be the same. There will always be little devils coming up, tempting you, saying, "Oh, you can do this." You have to learn, as Jesus did, that no matter how much you are offered to do something bad, you must be able to stand firm and say no.

Now, I'd like to have Herman show us how he says no. Herman is a powerful tool when I take him into my hand. I have a board here. I am going to put this board down (place on a good, solid base), and I am going to strike that board with a firm stroke. The board will not give, and Herman will not give.

Now watch this. (pastor whacks the board). There, you see, that was a firm stroke by Herman, and that is what we expect of you as you grow up. Stand firm for what is right.

Thank you, Herman. Boys and girls would you like to thank Herman?

We will be seeing Herman again next week.

SECOND SUNDAY IN LENT

Gospel Lesson: John 4:5-26
Key Word: **Proclamation**
Objects: Herman the Hammer
        Hand-printed sign with the words—I who speak to you am he
        Small tack and a place to put the tack

Here's our friend Herman the Hammer back again, ready to help us with the lesson today. Would you like to say good morning to Herman the Hammer? Now, before I begin, our word today is a big, long one, *proclamation.* Does anybody have any idea what proclamation means?

(Remember the original instructions, never press for an answer.) I didn't think any of you would know, so I am going to tell you. A proclamation is an announcement. I just made a proclamation when I told you what a proclamation is. Proclamation means, "I am going to tell you."

This lesson has two things to say to us, no matter how little or how big we are. The two main points of the lesson are: Jesus went to this woman who was just an ordinary person, no one special, and all alone. While he was talking to her he said, "I am Jesus, who has come to save the world. I am the Messiah." He didn't go out and find a big crowd. He came to this one woman, standing all alone by a well in Samaria, and he said to her, "I am Jesus." That was his first proclamation to this lady. Remember, he told her, "I am Jesus." And he does that to you every day. He does that to you especially every Sunday in church and in Sunday school. It is a reminder that Jesus is your friend.

After he talked to the woman by the well for a while, he finally ended by saying, "I who speak to you am he." Here is where we are going to need our friend and teacher Herman the Hammer. Often when you have a proclamation to make, you put it on a sign. You nail it up on the wall so that everybody can see it. That day Jesus made a proclamation that even now, years later, is important and worthwhile enough to put up a sign. Herman, would you put up our proclamation? (Minister tacks sign to anything convenient, then steps back. Herman, you did a good job of proclamation today. Now let me read it to the boys and girls. They can use it as their verse today. This is Jesus speaking, remember—"I who speak to you am he." This was his second proclamation to the woman at the well. Jesus is saying, "I am the Messiah. I am the one who is coming during this Lenten time." Remember the proclamation of Jesus. "I who speak to you am he."

Thank you, Herman. Would you like to say good-bye to Herman, boys and girls?

THIRD SUNDAY IN LENT

Gospel Lesson: John 9:1-41
Key Word: **Blind**
Objects: Herman the Hammer
        Two-by-four board, a foot long (was used two weeks ago)
        Nail (eight penny nail, which will be driven about one-half inch into the board before you start this sermon)
        Blindfold

Good morning, girls and boys. Time to say hello to our friend Herman the Hammer. Our word for today, one you probably know, is *blind.* Just what does this mean? Good! I thought one of you would know it (again, don't push, perhaps they will not know what the word means—just say, to be blind is to be unable to see).

Remember the gospel lesson for today is about a man who was born blind. This man heard that Jesus was coming through his town, and he stood by the side of the road. When he heard the crowd make noise he knew Jesus must be there. He cried out and said, "Jesus, help me! Jesus, help me! I am blind."

Today when someone is blind, we all feel sorry for that person. We try to help as much as we possibly can. But in those days, blindness was thought to be a punishment for sin. Either the person or the parents had done

49

something wrong; God was punishing them. Almost the only thing a blind person could do in those days was to become a beggar.

The blind man said to Jesus, "You can make me see." Jesus was impressed by the fact that this man believed in him, but he didn't say, "You can see." Instead he put some mud on the blind man's eyes and said, "Now go to the pool and wash the mud away." The man believed enough to go and do it. He did not think it silly, or useless. The man went to the pool, and when he washed away the mud he could see.

I am sure we all agree that being blind is not a very nice thing. So we are going to call on our friend Herman the Hammer. He will show us just how important it is to see. Remember, Jesus can show you the real, true light. I need a volunteer to help Herman.

Here is what we are going to do. We have a board with a nail already in it. All you have to do is take Herman the Hammer and, using your arm, put some of the power that Herman has into driving that nail into the board a little more. It doesn't have to go all the way through, just hit it a little bit more. Do you think you can do that? Good!

(Hand the child the hammer. Just before he or she is ready to pound the nail say, "Wait a minute." Take the blindfold and blindfold the child. Turn the child around once and ask that he hit the nail.) Obviously the child will be confused (don't let the confusion last too long). Like Jesus, I am saying, "you can see" (remove the blindfold). All right, now that you can see again, put some power behind Herman and let Herman show you how he can drive that nail into the board.

You are not really ready to go to work for Jesus until you can see. Herman did his job, once you could see.

Thank you, Herman.

FOURTH SUNDAY IN LENT

Gospel Lesson: Matthew 20:17-28
Key Word: **Servant**
Objects: Herman the Hammer
    Piece of string
    Pair of scissors

(Hang Herman from whatever is available, somewhere near the place where the children's sermon is delivered. Tie the string around the handle of the hammer and let Herman hang, hammer-side down. This will be done before the service starts so that when you begin the story, Herman is already hanging there.)

Our word for today is *servant*. Does anyone know what the word servant means? When your mother brings you your dinner, she serves the meal; that makes her the servant of that meal. Now, that is not a bad word, that is a good word. One of the things that made it such a good word is that Jesus, himself, in our lesson today said, "I am the servant. Anyone who wishes to be the master must first be a servant."

The mother in our lesson today brought her two sons to Jesus and said, "I would like you to make my two sons your chief disciples." Jesus told her that it was not quite that simple. If her sons were really going to be in charge, they had to be ready to do what he did. Would they be willing to die? If you cannot be a servant, you cannot be a master.

These two young men, who were brought to Jesus, weren't quite ready to die. They weren't even ready to be servants.

See what's hanging over there? You notice this morning I didn't say here's Herman, say good morning to Herman. See where Herman is hanging? He is hanging by a string, and Herman is power. Remember we talked about that? But do you know what? He's just hanging there, completely useless because Herman is really a servant. Unless somebody takes Herman by the handle, Herman just hangs there.

Now let's change Herman from a useless thing into a real servant. Watch (take the scissors and cut the string and let Herman loose).

For the past weeks now, boys and girls, we have been watching Herman do all sorts of things. This week Herman isn't going to do anything because we know what he can do already. Look what happened to Herman. Herman was just an old hammer, hanging at the end of a string. Now that I have cut the string, I can take a firm grip on the handle, and hold Herman in my hand, and suddenly Herman becomes a servant again. He can pound a board, he can drive a nail. He can do anything I ask him to do once again. Herman has the power to be a servant of God. Boys and girls, Herman did it again.

Do you want to say good-bye to Herman?

FIFTH SUNDAY IN LENT

Gospel Lesson: John 11:1-53
Key Word: **United**
Objects: Herman the Hammer
Three boards—preferably three pieces of lattice-strip (about 1 inch or 1⅛ inch wide and a foot long.) They will be placed on each side of the church about twenty feet apart, if that is possible. Herman is to be in the middle
A large nail

Our word for today is *united.* Does anyone know the meaning of united? United means "together." For instance, when you go to school, then come home, whether you walk home or take the bus, your mother meets you at the door, she grabs you and hugs you and says, "Welcome home." You are united. You are back together again.

The gospel lesson this morning was one of those long ones. Unless you listened very carefully, you probably said to yourself, "I don't think this will ever end." It was a very interesting story because Jesus was asked to raise a man from the dead. The man had been dead for several days. Jesus went to the village where his friend had died and saw the man's sisters crying. Jesus said to them, "Your brother will rise." That was hard to believe, but Jesus saw the sisters really believed that he could raise their brother from the dead. Remember, unless you believe Jesus can do it, he probably will not be able to help you. But, these sisters said, "If you tell him to come back to life, he will. You can unite us. You can bring our

brother back to us so we can all be together again?"
Jesus said, "Yes, I can."

(At this point, start to walk toward one of the little
boards that will be Lazarus.) Now I am going to the grave
and get Lazarus. Lazarus, come out (now walk all the way
across the church to the other little boards lying on the
floor and pick them up). These are Lazarus' sisters.
Jesus united Lazarus and his sisters, and Herman will
show us how it's done (at this point, you are back at the
center of the church. Pick up Herman and the nail. Tap
the nail through the boards. Hold up the three boards
that are now one). Jesus united Lazarus and his sisters
again. Herman has shown us what the power of God can
do—bring people back together again.

Time to say good-bye to Herman.

PALM SUNDAY
(Sunday of the Passion)

Gospel Lesson: Matthew 21:1-11
Key Word: **Parade**
Objects: Herman the Hammer
       A handful of small palm fronds

(Completely surround Herman with the fronds.
Probably the best thing to do would be to put them all
around the handle, and then use a rubber band or two so
that the fronds are secure when you pick up the
hammer.)

Our word for today is *parade*. Everybody loves a
parade. I am sure you all know what a parade is. Would
someone like to tell me what a parade is?

Excellent. That's what a parade is. We all love parades,

and that is what we are going to talk about this morning.

I know you have all seen a parade. There are parades with firemen, parades with soldiers and sailors; there are many different kinds of parades. The bands march and play music. The floats go by, people wave, and sometimes they even throw candy. It is always fun. We stand on the sidewalk as the bands, our friends, and the floats go by. We cheer and clap and say to each other that this is a wonderful parade. After it is over, we go back home and forget all about it.

That is the sort of thing that happened in the gospel lesson today. What a parade they had in Jerusalem that day! The people of the city spread palms on the road for Jesus; they waved other palms in the air. They even put their coats on the road for him to go over. They called, "Hosanna to the Son of David! Blessed is he who comes in the name of the Lord! Hosanna in the highest!" What a happy day that was! There was a great parade! When it was all over, some people wanted to take Jesus and make him the king. But Jesus went off and refused to become king. Then the people forgot about the parade.

S-a-aay, whatever happened to our friend, Herman? We haven't seen him yet today. Oh! there he is. Look at him. All dressed up for the parade. He is dressed in palms. Boys and girls, say good morning to Herman.

Herman got caught up in the spirit of the parade. He is excited about this day, Palm Sunday. You may be excited too, but will you boys and girls remember what today's parade was all about on Good Friday when Jesus died? And then again on Easter Sunday when he rose?

Let's see whether Herman is able to keep the spirit of the parade alive until next week. Let's see whether you boys and girls can keep the spirit of Palm Sunday and the joy of the parade, alive until next Sunday when we will meet Herman for the last time.

Would you like to say good-bye to Happy Herman today?

EASTER SUNDAY
(The Resurrection of Our Lord)

Gospel Lesson: John 20:1-18
Key Words: **Happy Easter, everyone! He is risen!**
Objects: Herman the Hammer
        Cymbal, triangle, little bell, pan—anything to make some noise and sound happy.

Well, boys and girls, here is our old friend Herman the Hammer. Today we don't have a word. We have quite a few words, but we will come to them in just a minute.

First, I'd like to tell you how much Herman has enjoyed being with you these last seven weeks. This is Herman's last day with us. During these six Sundays in Lent we have enjoyed seeing Herman in all sorts of moods. He has been strong, he has been blind. He has had all sorts of experiences during this Lenten season. We hope you have enjoyed him and have been able to learn from him. Remember last week Herman was at the parade on Palm Sunday? Now he is here on Easter Day. He is just as happy as can be that Jesus is risen from the dead. Herman wants to teach us his last and final lesson.

Herman, are you happy today? If you are show us (pastor now hits the cymbal, pot, bell, or anything to make some noise and happy sounds, with the hammer). Herman wants to tell you how happy he is, and he wants to leave you with this Easter thought.

Are you ready? *Happy Easter, everyone. He is risen!* Can you all say that with Herman? Let's try it. Here we go—*Happy Easter, everyone. He is risen!* Let's do it once more. Real loud now so everybody can hear it—*Happy Easter, everyone. He is risen!*

Thank you, Herman. You have been a good teacher all these weeks, and I am sure the children would like to say thank you and good-bye. All right, boys and girls, "Thank you and good-bye, Herman."

"Keep Looking Up"
(Seven Sundays after Easter)

This series of post-Easter sermons is entitled "Keep Looking Up." A little preparation will be necessary, but once you have put the materials together your objects are ready for the next seven weeks.

Objects Required

• Arrow cut from cardboard, about two feet long, hand lettered with the words KEEP LOOKING UP.

This sign is to be placed in a prominent spot in the church and left there for the seven weeks, so you can use it each Sunday.
· • art pad—fourteen-by-eighteen inches, or whatever size you can find.
• easel to hold the art pad (at least seven pages).
• box of crayons.
• older person or young adult with some art ability to assist you, or you may choose to do it yourself. You may even be fortunate enough to have a child who can do these simple drawings.

SECOND SUNDAY OF EASTER

Gospel Lesson: John 20:19-31
Key Word: **Believe**
Object: Rainbow

We are beginning a new series of sermons. For the next seven Sundays we will be watching an arrow as it shows us how to keep looking up and what to look for.

Let me show you what I mean. Here is our guide (put up the arrow)—KEEP LOOKING UP.

We will be following that arrow for the six Sundays after Easter and Ascension Day. We will come back to the arrow later. Now, let's get started.

Our key word is *believe*. Who knows what that means? That means "to accept as true or real—to know that something is true."

Now, in our gospel lesson today, what happened to Thomas? The other disciples said, "Jesus was here. We saw him." Thomas said, "I don't believe that."

That's pretty bad. After all the time Thomas had spent with Jesus, and he could say, I don't believe that.

You know, when your mom or dad or some adult person tells you something, if you should say "I don't believe that," they would get upset. They tell you they wouldn't lie to you. Your friends also don't like it when you say: "I don't believe that."

Jesus didn't like it either. He came back, and Thomas was there this time and Jesus said, "Thomas, I am sorry you don't believe. Now I'll prove it to you." Thomas replied "No, now I believe."

This is so great. When you and I sometimes have trouble believing, we can remember that Jesus forgave Thomas.

(Begin to make a rainbow on a pad) What is one of God's signs of forgiveness? A rainbow. We have a rainbow because that was one of God's signs that he forgives us. It is a sign from God in the sky. Keep looking up.

THIRD SUNDAY OF EASTER

Gospel Lesson: Luke 24:13-35
Key Words: **Eyes Opened**
Object: Stars at night

Jesus had just risen from the dead. Two men were walking along the road, and another man caught up with them and said hello.

Now watch this. "Their eyes were kept from recognizing him." Don't you think that is kind of strange? Why would Jesus do that? Their eyes were closed as they walked all day long, and they didn't know who he was.

Do you remember last Halloween when you and your friends got all dressed up. Sometimes when you saw one of your friends you probably didn't even know who that person was. Then all of a sudden your friend will laugh or smile or say something, and as soon as you hear or see that one little familiar thing you say, "Oh! that's Charlie, or Joe."

We all do things that give us away to our friends.

Jesus wasn't just trying to fool these men. He needed time to give them a message for all the disciples —that includes you and me, too.

Jesus wanted to say, "Everything that has happened and everything that will happen is just what the Bible said would happen. There are no surprises."

(You should start to draw some stars on your art pad) Did you ever sit outside as the sun was going down? First there is brightness, and then it slowly starts to get dark. As it gets dark, if you keep looking up you will see stars beginning to appear. First a few, and then more and more, until finally the whole heavens are covered with bright stars.

That is what happened to these men. Slowly they started to get this strange feeling about the man walking with them. As it got dark they could see more and more until the stranger "took the bread and broke it."

As their *eyes opened* fully, all the stars came out, they knew it was Jesus. They were so excited. Now they knew for certain he had risen. Keep looking up!

FOURTH SUNDAY OF EASTER

Gospel Lesson: John 10:1-10
Key Word: **Voice**
Object: Mountain

The key word today is *voice*. You all must know what a voice is. What is a voice? Good, now isn't it funny that the Gospel talks about sheep and shepherds, and our key word is *voice?*

I know you are all experts on voices. At night when you are supposed to go to sleep, but you don't, your dad says, "Settle down and go to sleep." You know that voice!

If you have a pet, a cat or dog or bird, that pet knows your voice. You call and it knows you.

Let me tell you a little bit about sheep so you will understand what Jesus was talking about (a mountain should be drawn on the art pad).

In those days there would be four or five shepherds, each with his own flock. To protect the sheep, they would all get together and build a fence. In the daytime the shepherds took the sheep up the mountain to eat grass; at night they were brought back down to a safe place. Now, all the sheep would get mixed up, hundreds of sheep all mixed up, belonging to five different shepherds.

In the morning each shepherd would call his sheep, and the sheep knew their own shepherd's voice. Each one followed his own shepherd.

That is why our word is *voice.*

We have to know the voice of our Shepherd, who is Jesus. When he calls we follow.

There was no grass in the valley so the shepherd led his flock up to the mountain to eat what they needed to grow strong.

Today, we look to the mountain where the grass is green and thick—keep looking up. Follow the voice of the Shepherd so you can have a good life too.

FIFTH SUNDAY OF EASTER

Gospel Lesson: John 14:1-12
Key Word: **Authority**
Object: The sun

Wait until you hear what our key word is for today! Even if you don't know what it means, you know how it works. Our word is *authority.* What is the best way for me to explain this? The dictionary says it is "the power to command or act." That doesn't help much.

OK, how about this? This will be just make-believe because I know none of you boys and girls would ever do this. All right? Just make-believe. Suppose you have just come home from school and your mother tells you to go and change your clothes before you go out to play. You tell her you don't have to, only your father can tell you what to do.

You had better be ready to duck, because you are about to find out that your mother does have the authority to command and act. You just watch her move. You may not have ever seen her move so fast.

That was just make-believe, but this is real. All of you have done something to test your mom and dad's authority. You disobey and perhaps they command, "Go to your room, you don't get your allowance this week."

That is what authority means, and you know that Mom and Dad have it. So does Jesus. He says, "When you have seen me, you have seen the Father." That is the authority God gave him.

(Start to draw a big, bright sun) See the sun—that is like God. Remember a couple of weeks ago we talked about when the sun goes down then you can see the stars. Today it is just the opposite; when the sun shines it blots out everything else.

The earth would die very soon if the sun stopped shining. People would die if God stopped shining in their lives. Keep looking up and let the Son show you the way and warm up your life.

Gospel Lesson: John 14:15-21
Key Word: **Commandments**
Object: Moon

Our key word today is a long one— *commandments.*
Can anyone tell me what that means? (You should get an
answer close enough to make it do.) Good, now we are
going to go to school for just a second to see what that
gospel lesson said. OK?

I looked it up in the dictionary to see exactly what this
meant. It said two things: "(1) One of the Ten
Commandments and (2) An order; direction; law."

Isn't it interesting how the dictionary can sometimes
help you understand what it says in the Bible?

Let me tell you what it says in the Gospel. Jesus said,
"If you love me, you will keep my commandments."

The dictionary says "Commandments," one of the
Ten Commandments.

Jesus gave the order. That makes it another
commandment, not just something someone said, like
"don't hit your brother or sister." That may be the law in
your house, and it is a good law, but this is *the* Law.

Remember our motto Keep Looking Up. Now is the
time. Jesus says, "I will not leave you."

(Start to draw a moon on your pad) Look up at the
moon. What happens to the moon in the daytime? Good
(if you get an answer—if not) It seems to fade away or
sometimes disappear. It doesn't really go away. It is still
there, the sun is so bright we can't see the moon's light.

"I will not leave you." That's what Jesus promised.
Sometimes it may be hard for us to see him. That is

because we moved away, he is still there. When our hearts and eyes get used to him again, he will be there. Keep looking up.

THE ASCENSION OF OUR LORD

Gospel Lesson: Luke 24:44-53
Key Words: **Wind and clouds**
Object: Wind clouds

Wind and *clouds*. These are two things we know about. Aren't they, boys and girls?

We have seen those dark clouds that look like big waves moving across a gray winter sky. The white ones usually mean a warm, pretty day. Then there are the black ones that mean a thunderstorm, or maybe even snow (some clouds should be being drawn on the art pad).

Clouds have a lot to do with our lives.

Wind is another thing we know all about, but we don't know anything about.

Did you hear what I just said? We know all about the wind, but we don't know anything about the wind.

We know what the wind does; in summer it makes us a little cool, in fall it blows the dry leaves about, in winter it piles up the snow, in spring it dries the wet ground. It must come from somewhere, I don't know where, do you?

One day Jesus was standing with his disciples, giving them some last instructions. Just like the coach at a football game before the game starts. "We can win; you are ready; let's go get them!" There was a gentle breeze, and it was a day with a beautiful, blue sky. Jesus just started to go up until he disappeared into a great white cloud. He was gone—back to his Father in heaven.

God uses the things of nature, such as wind, clouds, and the sky all through the Bible to help us understand him better.

White clouds, black clouds, gentle winds, strong winds. These all show us that God is here, now, saying, "Here is my blessing." Keep looking up.

SEVENTH SUNDAY OF EASTER

Gospel Lesson: John 17:1-11
Key Word: **One**
Object: Church steeple (very high)

Today we have a key word we just can't miss with. Everyone must know what *one* is.

If you ever saw a football game, you know that the team that wins always runs around holding up their right index finger and saying, we're number one! Let me see that number one finger. Hold it way up high so we all can see.

Now put your hands down for a minute. I want to tell you about number one as the church means it, not like the sports teams do. What is the difference, can anyone tell me?

Let me tell you then. Hold up your fingers showing we're number one again, real high. Fine, that's the sports number one. Hold it up and watch me do some magic. Ready, I am going to change those fingers from sports fingers to church fingers. Here we go—We are one. Did you get that? We are one. Hold those fingers up high. The last line of the gospel lesson says "That they may be one, even as we are one." We are one with God, and one with each other—we are all one.

You can put your hands down, but let's start looking up.

(Show a steeple that you have drawn on the art pad) See that church steeple? It looks as if it goes clear up to the sky. See what it has at the top. What is it? A cross! Right.

All over our town (or city), all over this state, all over our country, and all over this world, you will find churches with big steeples, little steeples, all with a cross at the top.

That tells us we are one." Let's see those fingers—all together now, "We are one." Don't ever forget it. If you need a reminder, when you pass a church just keep looking up.

Pentecost

(Group one—nine Sundays)

The twenty-eight Sundays after Pentecost are not set up in a series. To assist you in lining up the objects you will need for the sermons, we have arbitrarily divided them into three groups.

Here are the first nine.

Objects Required

- man with a mother, wife, and son
- rock
- handful of coins
- sign with THE KINGDOM OF HEAVEN IS AT HAND taped to a yardstick
- boy with a full head of hair
- cup of water
- father and son who look alike
- seeds
- weeds

THE HOLY TRINITY
(First Sunday after Pentecost)

Gospel Lesson: Matthew 28:16-20
Word: **Trinity**
Object: A man who has a mother, wife, and
son—all members

Our word today is *Trinity*. Who knows what that word means? That's a tough one.

Here is what the dictionary says, "Triple person, separate but united, composed of three persons." Well, now that we know what the dictionary says, I think you may still be a bit confused.

Let's try this. God was in the beginning (one). Then he sent his Son, Jesus (two). Finally, he sent his Spirit (three). That is three in one—God, Jesus, and the Holy Spirit. Are you still confused? Let's try one more time.

You remember in our gospel lesson Jesus told his disciples to go and make all of us disciples, which means "followers of Jesus."

We are to be baptized in the name of the Father (one); the Son (two); and the Holy Spirit (three). There we go again, one, two, three. That old triple play that is a trinity.

Here is something you can easily understand (have the father come forward). You all know Mr. So-and-so (have his mother come up). This is Mrs. So-and-so, you know her too (then have the son come forward). You all know so-and-so (have the wife come up). You all know Mrs. So-and-so.

(Ask mother) Who is this? "My son."
(Ask wife) Who is this? "My husband."
(Ask child) Who is this? "My father."
Holy Trinity! We understand at last.

If this man can be a son, a father, and a husband, he is really a trinity.

Holy Trinity—three in one.

That is the gospel truth.

SECOND SUNDAY AFTER PENTECOST

Gospel Lesson: Matthew 7:[15-20] 21-29
Key Word: **Sand**
Object: Rock

Our key word today is one you all know, *sand.* There is no need to ask whether you know what sand is? I will ask where you have seen sand? At the beach? Good. When workers build a house they use sand to make the mortar or cement. There is sand in the sandbox in your back yard or playground area. There is sand in the bottom of the fish tank. It's all around us.

We think we know what sand is don't we? But do we really?

Let me tell you a little about it. Sand is made by water wearing away at rocks for years and years. It takes such a long time. There are some rocks that are not too hard. These are known as sandstone. Over many years they are ground down and finally turn to sand.

In our Gospel today God said, "Don't be foolish and build your house on sand, it will just wash away." You know when you build sand castles at the seashore, and the tide comes in, the beautiful sand castles just collapse and disappear.

God says, "Be wise, build on a rock." (Hold up rock) That's hard, that will last. It will not wash away.

The winds blow, the rains come, and the tide comes in.

But if your house is built on a rock it will still stand.

If you hear when God tells you to be good, and you listen and are good, then you are on a rock. You will stand.

If you don't listen, then you are on sand. You will get into trouble.

Listen to God. Stand on a rock.

THIRD SUNDAY AFTER PENTECOST

Gospel Lesson: Matthew 9:9-13
Key Word: **Tax**
Object: Money

Do you know what *tax* means? That is our key word for today. I am certain your mom and dad know what tax means.

Tax is what we pay to the government. That is where the money comes from to pay the firefighters and the police, the mayor, and the president of the United States.

It is money we pay for the privilege of living here and living in America.

In the days of Jesus, everybody hated the tax collector. We don't hate our tax collectors today. We all may not like to pay so many taxes, but we don't hate the tax collector. Let me tell you why the tax collector in Jesus' day was disliked so much.

The Jewish nation was controlled by Rome. They were part of the Roman Empire. One of Rome's laws said that the people who lived there had to pay taxes. The Jewish people didn't like that. They didn't want to pay taxes to Rome; they wanted to be free.

The Rome governor picked a Jewish person they

could trust and made him the tax collector for his city. He collected the taxes and could keep some of all the money he collected. He made a lot of money (have a handful of coins ready).

All the other Jews said, "You are a traitor to your people. You work for Rome, and you take our money. You are as bad, no, worse, than the Romans. You are a Jew and a traitor to your own people. You take our money. We hate you."

So, all the people hated the tax collector.

In our Gospel today, Jesus walked up to a tax collector named Matthew and said, "Follow me." And Matthew did.

Jesus took this hated tax collector, Matthew, and turned him into Saint Matthew. The Saint Matthew who wrote this gospel lesson. He became one of the chief disciples.

Jesus is saying to you, right now, (show coins again), "Forget money, don't worry about a thing. Follow me." Why don't you try it?

FOURTH SUNDAY AFTER PENTECOST

Gospel Lesson: Matthew 9:35–10:8
Key Word: **Harassed**
Object: Sign with THE KINGDOM OF HEAVEN IS
AT HAND
(Have this sign taped to a yardstick and have a child walking back and forth holding up the sign.)

Harassed is our word for today. That is a tough one. It means "to bother by repeated attacks" or "to worry or scare."

The Jewish people were so upset by the Roman soldiers' threats and their bullying that they were just nervous wrecks.

The Roman soldiers had great power over the people. The people were always afraid of them.

If you were a Jew walking down the road and a Roman soldier was going the same way, he could just say to you, "Carry my packages." The law said you had to do this for one mile, no more. The Jewish people didn't like that at all.

The Jewish people were harassed. They were frightened and mistreated every day. I am certain we would not like to have to live that way.

Jesus went to preach and teach in the temples. He could tell that the people were very, very upset. He called his disciples and he said, "These things just have to stop. There are only twelve of you, so don't try to go everywhere at once, start with the Jews. Go tell them the good news."

Do you see what that sign says—THE KINGDOM OF HEAVEN IS AT HAND. That was the message those poor harassed people needed to hear. Go tell them!

The disciples went and started telling the good news. Now, two thousand years later, the message has not changed one little bit.

You still have to go, with your sign, into all the world that does not know Jesus and say, "The kingdom of heaven is at hand."

No one can harass or bother you. You don't have to be afraid. Jesus is here to help you.

FIFTH SUNDAY AFTER PENTECOST

Gospel Lesson: Matthew 10:24-33
Key Word: **Above**
Object: Hair (Have a boy with a full head of hair available.)

Our key word today is *above*. Someone must know what that means.

Above means "over" or "in a higher place." For example, you are upstairs in your room and your mom is down in the kitchen, you are above your mom.

When you move to a new class at school at the end of the year, you are one grade above last year's grade.

In our Gospel today Jesus tells us two stories.

First, a disciple is not above his teacher. You can be like your teacher, and that's enough.

I know when I was in school and also in church school, I always wanted to be like my teacher. I hope you all want to be like your teachers.

Just remember, we want to be like, not above, the people in our life that we love and respect. Parents, teachers, friends, and so many more.

Second (have a child come up front with you and ask), How many hairs do you have on your head? You don't know how many hairs you have on your head? Why, it's your head, didn't you ever sit and count them?

You know what? I know why you don't know. You are young. You just never thought to count them. I bet your mother will know the exact number. Let's ask her, "Mother, do you know how many hairs are on your child's head?"

You know, I think my grandfather may have known

how many he had. He was bald, and he may have been able to count them.

Do you know who knows how many hairs you have on your head? That's right, God knows. He cares for us, each one of us is precious in his sight. The Gospel says, "Even the hairs of your head are all numbered." That is why God is God. He knows each one of us by name. He cares for each one of us.

He will be with us every time we need him. He cares.

SIXTH SUNDAY AFTER PENTECOST

Gospel Lesson: Matthew 10:34-42
Key Word: **Righteous**
Object: Cup of water

Here is a word that sounds kind of hard, but when we look at it, it is really a simple word that we all know. The word is *righteous*. Do you know what that means? It sounds hard, but it means "doing right."

We all know what doing right means. When we do something good, our parents or teachers say, "That was very good." That is doing right.

In the Gospel it says good people should help good people.

We Christians should love each other. It should show in the way we treat each other. When we see another person do something good, we should go out of our way to encourage that person. We are to be kind.

Then Jesus said that giving even a cup of cool water was righteous (hold up the cup of water). Now, that doesn't sound like very much. You must remember, however, the Holy Land where Jesus was teaching was a very dry country, and water was often very scarce.

Even more scarce was cool water. This meant it had been drawn from a deep well and stored in a clay crock in the shade for very special occasions.

If you shared your cool water with a friend that was nice. If you shared your cool water with a stranger, you were doing something special, something righteous.

The righteous person gets a reward, and the person who shares a cup of cool water gets a reward too.

So, we who are disciples of Jesus, those of us who believe in Jesus, must look out for one another because we care about each other. Why? Because he cared for us first.

SEVENTH SUNDAY AFTER PENTECOST

Gospel Lesson: Matthew 11:25-30
Key Word: **Yoke**
Object: Father and son who look alike

Here is a word that comes from long ago, and you don't hear it used much anymore. It is the word *yoke*.

A yoke is a wooden frame to fit two oxen (a picture may help). There are two humps and two slings. You put one ox in each side, then hook the yoke of oxen to a wagon, and off you go; very slowly, oxen move very slow, you know, but off you go.

A yoke is for two oxen. Never one, always two. So, in our Gospel for today when Jesus says, "Take my yoke upon you," it means it takes two. Jesus is willing to be in the yoke with you. Are you willing to share (take on) his yoke? You will have to pull your share of the load, but with Jesus as your partner, it will always be easy.

Some people have trouble trying to understand how it is that if you see Jesus you see the Father (bring the father and son up to the front).

Let me show you how this can happen. Here is Mr. So-and-so and his son. I think they look so much alike that if Mr. So-and-so told us this wasn't his son, we wouldn't believe him.

We have seen how you can know the father by knowing the son. We have also seen that Jesus shows his love and concern for you by being willing to join you in the yoke, and so we see God as a loving concerned Father.

EIGHTH SUNDAY AFTER PENTECOST

Gospel Lesson: Matthew 13:1-9 [18-23]
Key Word: **Soil**
Object: Seeds

Our word today is an easy one; one we all know. It is *soil.* Sometimes we call it dirt, and we all know what dirt is.

I know you all go out to play with your little cars and trucks and build roads in the dirt. You race them all around in the dirt.

In the gospel lesson today, Jesus is thinking about dirt. It is really called soil. That's what we will call it today.

What Jesus is talking about is the soil where seeds are planted. He is talking about what kind of soil it is and how deep it is.

Here are some seeds. You all have seen seeds. Sometimes we plant flower seeds, and we get beautiful flowers. I think daisies are very pretty. Sometimes we plant vegetable seeds, and then we get corn or tomatoes or lettuce. Many, many vegetables are grown from seeds. What is your favorite vegetable?

Now when we plant this seed, it doesn't make any difference whether it is a flower or a vegetable. This seed will grow only if it has good soil and enough water and sun. If it has all these then you will have a beautiful garden: soil, seeds, water, and sun.

That is what Jesus is telling us in the story today.

You young people must never stop working on your growth as Christians. If you stop growing, you will die as a child of God.

This goes for all the people in this service today. I am talking to the children now, but you adults should listen too.

When Jesus says, "He who has ears, let him hear," he means you—all of you—big or little.

NINTH SUNDAY AFTER PENTECOST

Gospel Lesson: Matthew 13:24-30 [36-43]
Key Word: **Enemy**
Objects: Weeds

What is an *enemy?* A person who hates or tries to harm another is called an enemy.

I hope you children do not have any enemies. I know you may like some people more than you like others. I have some best friends, and some friends that are not as close; but I try not to have any enemies.

Just imagine if you had people who were your enemies. They hated you and wanted to harm you. That would sure scare you a little.

Jesus had a lot of enemies when he was on this earth. They hated him because they were afraid of him. They were bad people. They couldn't understand Jesus' talk about loving one another.

In the Gospel today, Jesus shows us what enemies can do.

There was a good man who went out to plant wheat. He was very careful. He put the wheat seeds in good soil. He took very good care of it. He was hoping to have a good harvest of wheat.

Now, this man had enemies who didn't want him to have a good harvest. In the middle of the night they crept into his fields and threw weed seeds in with the grain. A whole lot of weed seeds.

Now, when you cut wheat you expect a few weeds. Most of the weeds you pull out as you see them growing in with the good wheat.

If there are too many weeds you can't pull them all, so you just have to let them grow with the wheat. The weeds kill off a lot of the wheat, so you do not have a good harvest.

That is just what happened. The bad men ruined the harvest for the good man.

Here is what Jesus has to say about this. These weeds (hold up weeds) cannot be part of my harvest. Throw them in the fire and burn them. But the good grain, that will go in my barn and I will keep it.

Don't be my enemy, be my friend. Don't sow weeds, sow good seeds.

That is what God expects of each of us. He wants each of us to be a sower of good seeds.

Pentecost
(Group two—nine Sundays)

Here are the objects you will need for the second nine Sundays.

Objects Required

- pearl
- bread
- barometer
- tin cup
- three children
- a cross
- two pieces of rope, each three feet long
- ten-dollar bill and a dime
- two boys and two dimes

TENTH SUNDAY AFTER PENTECOST

Gospel Lesson: Matthew 13:44-52
Key Word: **Kingdom**
Object: Pearl

Our word today is *kingdom.* That's not such a hard word. A kingdom is a country ruled by a king.

If you look up the word "kingdom" in the dictionary that is just what you will read. There is another definition, however. It reads, "the domain over which God rules in heaven and on earth."

That is not from the Bible, that is from the dictionary. That is a very good explanation of what we mean in the Gospel when we read, "The kingdom of heaven is like a treasure hidden in a field."

The kingdom of God is here for all the boys and girls, everyone. But it is not free. God wants us all to want to be with him in his kingdom. He wants us to be willing to give up all we have to follow him.

In the first story, the man sold all he had to buy the field that had the treasure he wanted.

In the second story, the man discovered a very valuable pearl. He sold all that he had to buy it.

A pearl starts as a grain of sand in the shell of an oyster. If you have ever been out for a walk, and you get a stone in your shoe, you know how much that hurts. You stop, take off your shoe, and dump out the stone.

That is what the oyster tries to do. That grain of sand hurts. The oyster keeps coating the grain of sand with carbonate of lime. The coating keeps growing, until it is a pearl. If it is a perfect pearl it is worth a lot of money. If you want it, you have to be willing to pay for it.

This is why God's kingdom is compared to a treasure

or a perfect pearl. God's kingdom is the perfect prize. We should all be willing to give up all we have to get it.

"The domain over which God rules is heaven and on earth." That is the treasure, that is the perfect pearl. That is what we all want more than anything else in the whole world.

ELEVENTH SUNDAY AFTER PENTECOST

Gospel Lesson: Matthew 14:13-21
Key Word: **Compassion**
Object: Bread

Our word today is really a great word for you young people to learn. It is *compassion.*Let me tell you why it is such a great word. You probably do not know what it means.

I am sure we would all agree that compassion means to feel sorry for someone, and that is pretty close. In the gospel lesson today the disciples said to Jesus, "It is almost dark. Send the people away to find some food in the nearby town." I think this shows that the disciples felt sorry for all those people. The people had been with them all day and surely they were getting hungry. The disciples were good men, they didn't want to see anyone suffer or go hungry. They took the problem to Jesus.

Remember I said the disciples felt sorry for the people, but they were not compassionate, they just felt sorry. Jesus was immediately compassionate.

This is what compassion really means, "to feel sorry for another person and to help."

See this bread? The bread showed that Jesus was compassionate. He didn't just feel sorry for the people, he helped. He gave them bread and fish. He didn't send them away.

Because Jesus showed us the way, now we, all of us, boys, girls, and parents have to stop only feeling sorry for the poor and hungry people of the world. We have to take the bread and feed them. That is Christ's way.

I just love that word "compassion." It is an action word. It makes us do something, not just sit and feel sorry for the world.

TWELFTH SUNDAY AFTER PENTECOST

Gospel Lesson: Matthew 14:22-33
Key Word: **Fear**
Object: Barometer

Today we have a little change from our usual order. You know how I often say, here is the word. Do you know it? Today I think you will all know the word, but you may not know our object for today. Let's see how we do, OK?

The key word is *fear*. We all know what that means. Some of us older people, as well as you young ones, are afraid of thunder and lightning. Some are afraid of the dark, and some of us are afraid of being alone. We all know what it is to be afraid of something, and it is no fun to be in fear of anything, ever. Well, we all know what our word means, now let's see about our object.

Who knows what this is? (hold up barometer). That's great. It is a barometer. (if they don't guess, just tell them).

What does a barometer do? It tells us what the weather will be in the next day or so.

According to our gospel lesson for today the disciples

needed a barometer. When they set out in the boat the weather was nice. Then a storm came up, and they were all in fear for their lives.

When we are afraid we call on Jesus. Before the disciples had a chance to call Jesus was there, walking on the water.

Poor old Peter. He was always so ready to show his faith. He was also very human. He had so much faith he said, "Let me walk on the water out to meet you," and Jesus said, "Come on." And Peter did.

Just as he got near to Jesus, his fear grew bigger than his faith, and he started to sink.

Jesus saved him, but he also told him how disappointed he was. "O, man of little faith, why did you doubt?"

This is what he says to you, boys and girls. You don't have to be afraid ever, if you have faith. And that applies to you parents too.

THIRTEENTH SUNDAY AFTER PENTECOST

Gospel Lesson: Matthew 15:21-28
Key Word: **Begged**
Object: Tin cup (such as a measuring cup)

Our key word is *begged.* You all know what that means. It means "to ask over and over." Just one more piece of candy? or "Let me play just a few more minutes?" or "One more small cookie please?" That's begging!

Now in the Bible we almost always think of a beggar as a person with a tin cup (hold up cup), sitting by the side of the road calling out, "Help the poor!" All through the Bible there are many stories about beggars.

Today we find a lady who begged for something from Jesus, but she did not wave a tin cup. She called out, "Help me." We also see the disciples who begged something from Jesus, and they did not have cups either.

The lady begged Jesus to make her daughter well. Jesus did not perform a miracle of healing until the woman proved her faith. He said to her, "You are not even one of us, why should I heal your daughter?" The lady begged Jesus again and said, "Even the dogs eat the crumbs from the table."

Then the disciples begged for something else. They said, "Send her away, she is bothering us." It was too late. Jesus saw in this woman the proof of the faith that he needed. He said, "Your faith is so great, your daughter is healed."

The lady begged and showed faith. Jesus didn't even know her, but he knew faith when he saw it. He did this to show his disciples a lesson. The lesson is just as true for you today. You can be a beggar with a tin cup or a beggar with faith.

Your faith can make you whole and well.

FOURTEENTH SUNDAY AFTER PENTECOST

Gospel Lesson: Matthew 16:13-20
Key Words: **Who Am I**
Objects: Three children

For this lesson, I don't know whether to start with the word or the object. I know what I'll do. I'll do them both at once.

I would like to have three children, about five or six years old, come up here to help me. Fine. Now I'll stand here, and you stand in a line next to me and face all the people in the church.

Now we are ready to start. The key words are *Who Am I?* So I will start by asking, "Who am I?" "I am the Reverend _____. I am pastor of this church." Then you, starting at this side of me, say, "Who am I?" and then you tell us. (At this point the children may need a little help. You may need to say out loud, "Hold it, I have to do some coaching." Then whisper to the child, "Say what I say"—My name is_____. My mother and father are Mr. and Mrs. _____. I go to _____ school and am in _____ grade.)

Now this little game we just played is called Who Am I. Jesus did this with his disciples. He asked them who they thought he was. It was not a game with him, however. He wanted to know what these men, who had been with him for so long would answer. Who was Jesus?

They all had different answers. Just like we had different answers. They told him what other people said about who he was.

Then Jesus said, "Who do you say I am?" Jesus asked his disciples that question, but he also asks us today. "Who do you say I am?"

Can you answer with Peter, "You are the Christ."

If you can answer that question in that way, you have learned your lesson today.

FIFTEENTH SUNDAY AFTER PENTECOST

Gospel Lesson: Matthew 16:21-26
Key Word: **Rebuke**
Object: Cross

Our word today is *rebuke.* That means "to express disapproval," or to put it so we all understand, it means "to say sharply something is wrong."

Jesus is starting to prepare his disciples for the fact that he is going to Jerusalem and that he will be put on trial and crucified.

We talked several weeks ago about how Peter was always the first of the disciples to say or do something in response to what Jesus said.

Here he goes again. As soon as Jesus said "I will go and I will die," Peter just exploded, "God forbid, Lord, this shall never happen to you." And Jesus rebuked Peter sharply. Why did he speak to Peter like that? Peter didn't say anything wrong. He was trying to show his love for Jesus. Since he was the biggest and strongest of all the disciples, he was ready to fight to protect Jesus.

See boys and girls, it is so easy to say the right thing, but it is not always easy to do the right thing.

Jesus knew they were just words. When the time came for him to face the cross, he would be all alone.

Then Jesus said to Peter and to all the others, "Just words are not enough. If you are afraid to die, then you cannot follow me. If you try to save your life you will lose it."

See this cross (hold up the cross). This is what Jesus offered to his disciples that day. They heard what he said, but they did not understand it.

Not until later (hold up cross again), when they were all

afraid for their own lives and they saw Jesus hanging on the cross did they understand what he said to them that day.

Boys and girls, and all of you who hear this, it is still the same. We still have to take up our cross to follow him.

SIXTEENTH SUNDAY AFTER PENTECOST

Gospel Lesson: Matthew 18:15-20
Key Word: **Listen**
Object: Two pieces of rope (each three feet long)
        Scissors

Our word today is one we all know— *listen.* For some reason when we are small we are supposed to be good at listening. We listen in school, we listen to our parents, we listen to our minister, we listen to our friends. It just goes on and on.

When we are a little older, we don't seem to be as good at listening. In fact some of us talk so much it seems we never listen.

In the Gospel today Jesus talks about two friends, he calls them brothers. But he doesn't mean brothers in one small private family. He means brothers in a great big family that goes beyond private ones. We are all members of the family of this church. That makes us all brothers and sisters.

Now if two friends have an argument, they should not let it break up their friendship or upset the church family. Jesus says to settle it right away and not let the argument grow.

Sometimes when you have a fight with your friend you say something like, "I'll never speak to you again!" When this happens, if you don't make up soon, you discover your friend doesn't even miss you anymore. He's forgotten about you, and that makes you very sad. You have lost a good friend.

The thing we must learn to do, not just the children, but all of us, is to learn to say I am sorry. Let's forget about our silly arguments and start over. That way we can still be friends.

Your church is just like you, because it is you, and you, and you. We are the church. If we are angry with each other, then our friendship ends. We are unhappy, but so are the people around us.

Let me show you how we should be (take two pieces of rope, hold them up and tie them). Here are two people, we tie them together in God's family, with God's love, and now they are one. They have a fight (untie rope). They are two again (cut each rope in half). Look what happened. Now there are four people split by the fight.

Let's take this whole ball of rope (gather rope into your hands). I will hold it up high, and say I'm sorry. Let us forgive one another and get back together again (retie the pieces together). Now we are one again. That is what God wants for us—to be brothers and sisters who listen to each other.

SEVENTEENTH SUNDAY AFTER PENTECOST

Gospel Lesson: Matthew 18:21-35
Key Word: **Forgive**
Objects: A ten-dollar bill and a dime

How many times should we *forgive?* That is our word for today—forgive.

Do you have an idea what it means. It means that even if you did something I didn't like, I don't want to get even. It's OK. You are my friend. I understand and I forgive you.

Just suppose someone does something really bad, not just once, but many times. I guess you don't mind saying I forgive you one time, or maybe even twice, but enough is enough! You finally get to the place where you say, "No more. I have had it, that's enough!"

That is just what the disciples thought. In fact, they went by the old Jewish law that said you had to forgive seven times. They even asked Jesus if it was right to forgive seven times. Jesus gave them a new law. The new law said, not seven times but seventy times seven. Now that is a lot of forgiving. Jesus then went on to tell his disciples a story so they could understand what he meant.

A man owed his boss ten dollars (hold up the ten-dollar bill). Now that is a lot of money. The boss said he wanted the man to pay what he owed him. The poor man didn't have the money, and he told his boss that he didn't know whether he would ever be able to pay it back. He begged the boss to forgive that debt, not to make him pay. The boss felt sorry for the man and told him that he would forget it. The poor man would not have to pay him back. The man said, "Thank you, thank you, you are so kind."

On his way home, this man, who had been forgiven, met a man who owed him ten cents. He demanded that the man pay him his ten cents (hold up the dime). The man said that he didn't have any money and begged for mercy. He promised to pay as soon as he could.

The first man said, "That's not good enough. I want my money now, or I'll call the police and have you put in jail."

The first poor man did not learn to forgive, and the boss said, "Just as you did not forgive, I will not forgive, I will have you put in jail." Jesus wants us to forgive other people just as he forgives us.

How many times do you have to forgive? Don't ask me, ask Jesus. he said 490 times, at least. By then you will be pretty good at forgiving.

EIGHTEENTH SUNDAY AFTER PENTECOST

Gospel Lesson: Matthew 20:1-16
Key Word: **Denarius**
Object: Two children and two dimes

A *denarius* is a small gold or silver coin worth ten copper pennies. That was the kind of money they used in Jesus' time; it was Roman money.

Now the gospel story about the man in the vineyard is just not fair. This man has a big field full of grapes, all ripe and ready to be picked. He went out early one morning and hired some men to pick the grapes, promising to pay a denarius. Then three more times, later in the day, he went out and hired some more men to help pick the grapes. He paid each of them a denarius. Here is where we have a problem with the story. Let me show you what I mean. I would like two children to come up here who would like to make a dime (have two children come up front, but just as they get up stop one and say), "You can't just walk up here and get a dime that easy. I want you to walk down that side aisle, across the back, down the other side, and then come back here to me." Turn to the other child and say, "I asked you if you would like to make a dime, here it is."

When the other child gets back from the trip around the church say, "I just gave _____ a dime, and he (or she) didn't do anything. He just came up and I gave it to him. Now, after the walk you took,_____, how much do you think you should get? (If he says more than a dime) Sounds fair to me. (If he says a dime) I think maybe you understood the gospel lesson for today. You see, I have two dimes. They are mine. I can do whatever I want with them. I asked for two children who wanted to make a dime. I paid each a dime. One worked for it and one didn't. The reason it's fair is that I kept my word. I paid what I said I would pay.

That is what happens to us. Some of us are bad. We say I'll be good when I get older, then I'll get to heaven. Others say I'll be good now, then I will surely get to heaven. Jesus says, "No matter how long you work at it, it is my gift to give, and I will decide who comes to live with me." It is my dime; I'll decide who wins the prize in the end.

Pentecost

(Group three—ten Sundays)

Here are the objects you will need for the final ten Sundays of Pentecost.

Objects Required

- pitcher of water and two glasses
- bunch of grapes
- dish of candy
- one-dollar bill
- two Bibles
- one candle; two boxes of matches—
  one wet, one dry
- quarter
- organ or piano
- sign—The End
- plate of cookies

NINETEENTH SUNDAY AFTER PENTECOST

Gospel Lesson: Matthew 21:28-32
Key Word: **Will**
Object: Pitcher of water and two glasses

Our key word is *will,* and it can have many different meanings. It could be a boy's name. It could mean how you leave your money when you die; you make a will. It could mean you intend to do something, like when you say "I will do so-and-so."

The will we are talking about today is the will that means "I desire you to do something" or "I ask you to do something."

A father had two sons and he said to them, "Will you do something for me?" One son said no, but he did it, at last. The other son said sure, but he did not do it. Jesus asked which of the two did the will of his father?

I would like two children to come and help me (have two children all set to act out their parts as follows).

Give each child a glass. (To #1) I have a question for you. Will you hold this glass so I can pour some water in it? The child says, "No, I don't think so," and turns his back on the pastor.

(To #2 child) I have a question for you. Will you hold this glass so I can pour some water into it? "Sure," he says. (As you start to pour just a very little, since it will go on the floor, he pulls the glass away. Water falls on the floor. At this point #1 child says, "I changed my mind, I'll help." He holds out his glass and you fill it.)

Which of these children do you think did what I asked them? The one who said no, but then did what he was asked, or the one who said yes, then didn't do it?

What Jesus is saying in this gospel lesson is this.

Some people hear what the Bible says and they say, "I believe it," but they don't act like they believe it. Other people don't understand what the Bible says, but when they do understand, they believe it.

Boys and girls, don't just learn what Jesus is saying, live it. That is how you do the will of the Father.

TWENTIETH SUNDAY AFTER PENTECOST

Gospel Lesson: Matthew 21:33-43
Key Word: **Tenant**
Object: Grapes

What is a *tenant?* Does anyone know? A tenant is "a person who lives on another person's land and pays rent for living there."

Do you think we still have tenant farmers today like the one in the lesson? We certainly do. All over this country there are people who farm like that. Some are still called sharecroppers, because they share the crop with the person who owns the land.

The man in the story today must have built a pretty nice vineyard. It had everything that was needed to go into business. He found a good tenant, turned the place over to him, and then moved away, far away.

He knew when the grapes would be ripe (hold up a bunch of grapes). These sure do look pretty, all ripe and ready to eat. He sent his servants to get his share, but when they got there the tenant said, "The owner is a long way from here, why should I share with him? I did all the work." The servants were killed, and the tenant thought that was the end of that. But more servants showed up to get the owner's share, and they were killed too. So far all we have talked about is a bad tenant and a beautiful bunch of grapes. Listen to what happens next. The owner of the land said, "I'll send my son, they wouldn't dare do him any harm." Doesn't that sound a little like another story we know? Does anybody know who sent his son?

That's right. God sent his son. So, this whole lesson isn't about a tenant and grapes. It is about us.

How do we receive Jesus when he comes to us? Do we try to send him away?

It says very clearly, "If you don't accept the Son when he comes to you, he will go to someone who will accept him."

These grapes help us understand, but it is God we are really talking about. Accept him now!

TWENTY-FIRST SUNDAY AFTER PENTECOST

Gospel Lesson: Matthew 22:1-10 [11-14]
Key Word: **Feast**
Object: Dish full of candy

What is a *feast?* Do you know? At least this word is easy to explain. What happens at Thanksgiving time? All your friends or relatives get together for dinner. You have turkey, gravy, potatoes, stuffing, cranberries, pumpkin pie, fruit, and many other things. Oh, what a meal! By the time you get up from the table you are so full you can hardly move. Well, that's a feast!

The lesson tells us about a king who prepared a feast for his son's wedding. After everything was ready he invited all the guests to come and join him, but they started to make all kinds of excuses—they were too busy. This made the king very angry. Did you ever try to do something nice for a person, and it didn't turn out at all? Let me show you. Let's see, look at what I have here (hold candy dish). A nice dish of candy. Do I like candy! How about you boys and girls, do you like candy? I knew you would.

Now, I think I'll give this candy to the choir (let the choir members know you are going to do this and have them refuse to take any of the candy. Use excuses like: I'm on a diet, that's not the kind I like, too early in the day, not hungry, etc. These answers come one at a time as you offer the candy dish down the first row. Turn back to the children.

All right, if you don't want it, then I'll have my friends, the children, come up. They will like it. (Make sure the candy is small, wrapped pieces, to be eaten later. Have the children come up and take a piece of candy.) Thank you for coming to my candy feast.

Do you understand what just happened? Just like in our Gospel today, when the feast was ready, the guests were not ready. So the King, that's God, said to give it to the people who want it.

Boys and girls, you have just received a piece of candy. God has much more to offer. When he calls you, be ready. Don't let him offer your gift to anyone else. His gift is especially for you. Be ready to accept it.

TWENTY-SECOND SUNDAY
AFTER PENTECOST

Gospel Lesson: Matthew 22:15-21
Key Word: **Entangle**
Object: A one-dollar bill (In God We Trust)

The key word today has two meanings as it is used in the gospel lesson. *Entangle* means "to get twisted up and caught." That's exactly what these men were trying to do to Jesus. That's what the word means, and you can see that is what it means in the Gospel. The people did not ask this question to get to know what Jesus thought about a matter, they just wanted to get him in trouble. Jesus knew this, and, boy, was he ready for them (take out a one-dollar bill and hold it up). You can't see this too well, but your mom or dad can show you when you get home. This is a dollar bill and there is something on it—the great seal of the United States and the words In God We Trust.

A lot of people get all mixed up about what this Gospel says. If your mother said to you, "Go out and play. Stay out as long as you want. When you are really tired come in, and then you can do your homework."

You would probably say, "Are you sure you mean that? It's all backward. First I should do my homework, then go out to play."

People keep getting this lesson all mixed up and backward, then they have trouble understanding it. If you read it "Give to God the things that are God's," that's like doing your homework first, before you go out to play.

If you give to God what is God's, that means you support your church; you use some of that In God We Trust and send it back to God. Then you are doing what

God expects you to do. If you do all this first, then you will be a good citizen and "render unto Caesar the things that are Caesar's." That means you pay your taxes, like all good people do.

You see, just get your life in the right order, then all the rest will turn out all right. Put God first. It is as simple as that.

TWENTY-THIRD SUNDAY AFTER PENTECOST

Gospel Lesson: Matthew 22:34-40 [41-46]
Key Word: **Commandment**
Object: Two Bibles—One opened to the Ten Commandments (Exodus 20:1); the other to the gospel lesson for the day.

Commandment is a big word, but I think someone will know what it means. It means "an order or law," like the Ten Commandments. They are the ten laws that God gave the Jewish people through Moses. They are laws to live by.

Here is a funny thing about the laws that God gave in the Bible. I'm going to read you the Ten Commandments for our children's sermon today. I doubt if many of you have ever heard them read straight through like this. I'm not going to just read them so you can say, I heard them once. I'm doing this so I can ask you a question when I'm finished. So listen closely (read from the Bible).

What did each commandment say right away? Each had one common thing in it. Want to take a guess? Here it is, each one says, "You shall *not.*" That was the law that God gave to Moses and his nation in the Old Testament.

101

Now, from the Gospel for today I am going to read verses 37-40. See if you can see the difference between the old commandments in the Old Testament and the new commandments in the New Testament. Here we go, listen very carefully (read from the Bible).

Did you catch the great big difference? In the Old Testament the law says, "You shall not."

In the New Testament—the Gospel, the Good News—it says you shall do something—love.

See what happened to the message after Jesus came to earth? Not just the old law, "Do not," but the new law, "Love God, love man."

Let's see all the boys and girls in this church practice this new commandment this week. Love God; love one another?

TWENTY-FOURTH SUNDAY AFTER PENTECOST

Gospel Lesson: Matthew 25:1-13
Key Word: **Foolish**
Objects: Candle; wet matches, dry matches

I just know you know what the word *foolish* means because we have all been foolish, many times. It means "unwise, not too smart." We all have done things and later said "That wasn't too smart." That is what foolish means.

In our gospel lesson Jesus is the bridegroom, and we are the maidens. Some of us are wise and some of us are foolish. We just don't know when Jesus is coming back to earth, or perhaps just to visit us. We must be ready, however.

Let me show you what I mean. I need two children, old enough to light a match for me (have children come up).

Here is a candle that will represent the lamps in the story. What we are told in this lesson is what every Scout has learned, be prepared.

At home we are to have a flashlight ready in case the lights go out. We are supposed to have a battery-operated radio in case of emergency, so that if the power goes off, we can still get the news. What this means is, be prepared.

The lesson uses ten maidens waiting for the bridegrom to come. When he did come five of the maidens were prepared and five were not. Jesus said, "Those of you who are prepared, come with me."
We, here, are all prepared. We have our candle, it has a good wick and is all set to burn for us when we need it. So let's light it. Here are some matches. Light the candle (hand a pack of book matches that you have dipped in water to one of the children helping you). Well, we seem to have a problem. Maybe we were not as prepared as we thought we were. Let's not give up. Here I have some more matches, why don't you try it? (Hand dry matches to other child. The match lights, the child lights the candle.) "You were prepared."

This is what the lesson says, "Be prepared." You never know when you might meet Jesus. Get your life ready so when you strike, you light.

Gospel Lesson: Matthew 25:14-30
Key Word: **Afraid**
Object: Quarter

Here we come to another of those words that we all know well. Whether you are a child or a grown-up, you know that it is to be *afraid*. Have you ever been on a roller coaster—one of those rides that goes up and down, and every time it comes down the riders scream because they are afraid?

I hope none of you children has ever seen any of those horrible ghost movies. I really don't understand why anybody goes to see them. They promise to scare you to death. I don't want to be scared, and especially to death.

Can you imagine in our Gospel today, the Master, that's God, saying to you, "Take this talent and use it for me"? Would you say to God, "No, I'm afraid of you"? We are to love God, not to be afraid of him.

The first two men took what God gave them and said, "All right, God, thank you. We will just go to work and see what we can do for you." They did very well, and God was pleased with how they used the talents he gave them.

Fear stopped that third man. Have you ever been afraid, so afraid you could not even move? You were just frozen in fear. That can happen. That is what happened to this man who was given the one talent. God hoped he could handle just the one talent, but because he was afraid, he couldn't even handle that.

I have here a quarter. Let us say that this is the one talent God gave you to invest in his Kingdom. What would you do with the quarter so that if God came back a year from now and said, "How did you use the talent I gave you?" you could make God proud of you?

Put it in the offering at Sunday school?

Give it to feed the hungry around the world?

Give it to the Salvation Army?

Give it to help a missionary?

Give it to a poor man?

Give it to the Red Cross?

Whatever you do with it, if you give your all to help God's world or his poor people you will be doing the right thing. And God will be able to say, "You have used your talents well, I am pleased with you."

TWENTY-SIXTH SUNDAY AFTER PENTECOST

Gospel Lesson: Matthew 23:1-12
Key Word: **Practice**
Object: Organ or Piano

(This object must be set up in advance with your organist or pianist. Have organist/pianist to play a few bars of a familiar hymn with discords all through it. Then have the organist play it again perfectly.)

Now this is a word and a gospel lesson that makes me very nervous. The key word is *practice,*and the lesson is about preachers and church leaders who talk but do not act. It is about people who do their good deeds and their charity, not for people who need it, but so that men can see them doing these good things and say, "Isn't he a good man."

Boys and girls, if you are ever thinking about being a minister this gospel lesson points out one of the most frightening things about being a minister. You have to get up here Sunday after Sunday and tell your people how to think, what to do, how to live, and still you have to live with these people, and you are just as human as they are.

You have to practice what you preach. How can I show you boys and girls what I mean when I say You have to practice what you preach? I'm sure you all know that to play the piano or organ well takes a lot of practice. You just can't sit down and say, "I think I'll play the organ for the people at my church." We would love to have you want to play for us, but first you must practice. If you practice, when you sit down to play for us, you will be ready. We will enjoy your sermon in song. But first you must practice.

Suppose (Mr. or Mrs.) So-and-so, our organist (or pianist) didn't practice. How would it sound? Can you show us? (The organist plays discorded music.) That was awful! You must practice before you preach. Now are you ready to try again? (Now organist plays perfect tune.) That is perfect. We can tell that you have practiced, now you are not humbled but exalted.

TWENTY-SEVENTH SUNDAY AFTER PENTECOST

Gospel Lesson: Matthew 24:1-14
Key Word: **Heed**
Object: The End (sign)

In the gospel lesson today there is a word that we don't use much anymore. It is an old-fashioned word that your grandmother might use, but you don't hear it often. It is *heed.* Jesus said, "Take heed." That means "to pay attention" or "to notice."

Now that is simple enough. Your teacher probably didn't tell you last week to take heed, but I am sure your teacher said, "Pay attention," or "You had better notice what is going on here."

Our lesson today is on a subject that I know you are experts on. The subject is The End. The other night perhaps you wanted your mother to read a story before you went to bed. She read you the story, and when it was over she closed the book, gave a big sigh, and said, (hold up the sign) The End. Those words come at the end of a lot of things. Books often say it. Sometimes it is at the end of your favorite television show. It is always at the end of a movie. It says, The End (hold up the sign).

You know there are other ways to say The End. When two friends part, they shake hands. When you are finished talking on the telephone, you say good-bye.

When you see a train go by, it does not say The End on the back; you see the caboose, then you just know it's the end.

When people run a race, there is a tape stretched across the finish line, when the first person breaks the tape, that is the end.

When a football game is over they don't hold up a sign that says The End. They shoot off a gun.

In the lesson Jesus tells us all the things that will happen on earth, and then he says, "Then the end will come."

Take heed (hold up sign). The end will come.

LAST SUNDAY AFTER PENTECOST

Gospel Lesson: Matthew 25:31-46
Key Word: **Separate**
Object: Plate of Cookies

Our key word is a word that we older people know very well, but you boys and girls may not hear it much.

When some of us were growing up we used to separate boys' Sunday school classes and girls' Sunday school classes. In school we had a line for girls and a line for boys. That's our word for today, *separate.*

We no longer try to separate things, we try to make things equal. Let us think about *separate*

God thinks of us all as equal in his sight, but when he comes to earth again he will be ready to separate his people from those who chose not to follow him.

How can we tell who is a follower and who is not? Is there anyone here, who was here last week that remembers the test from last week's children's sermon? Remember the test Jesus had last week was, "Don't listen to what they say, look at what they do," or as we say, "Actions speak louder than words."

This is the last Sunday of the church year. Next Sunday will be the First Sunday of Advent. That is the start of the new church year.

I think there is a real message here for you boys and girls. As we end the church year, the last two gospel lessons say, "Don't just talk, do!"

(Take the plate of cookies that have been placed so the children can see it during the entire talk. You may even want to go pick one up as if you were going to eat it.)

Oh, I'm sorry. I have these delicious cookies here, and I almost forgot to ask if you would like to have one. Here, have one (pass the plate around).

When I was hungry, you fed me. When I was thirsty, you gave me drink. When I was naked, you gave me clothes.

The cookie I just gave you is a symbol of what God expects of us. Don't just talk. Do. God expects us to take care of each other. We are our brothers' and sisters' keeper. God will come someday to separate those who just talk from those who do. Speak up for Jesus. Make your actions and your life speak louder than your words.